YESTERDAY'S CARS

Superwheels & Thrill Sports

YESTERDAY'S CARS

PAUL R. DEXLER

Lerner Publications Company ■ Minneapolis, Minnesota

ACKNOWLEDGMENTS: All of the photographs in this book
have been provided by the author. The author wishes to thank
Robert E. Turnquist for his information about the Packard on
pages 18 and 21.

LIBRARY OF CONGRESS CATALOGING IN PUBLICATION DATA

Dexler, Paul R.
    Yesterday's cars.

    (Superwheels and Thrill Sports)
    SUMMARY: Introduces antique, classic, and
special interest cars, their restoration, and old car
collecting and competitions.

    1. Automobiles—Collectors and collecting—
Juvenile literature.   [1. Automobiles—Collectors
and collecting] I. Title. II. Series.

TL7.A1D48   629.22'22'075   79-1462
ISBN 0-8225-0420-0

Manufactured in the United States of America.

Published simultaneously in Canada by J.M. Dent & Sons
(Canada) Ltd., Don Mills, Ontario.

International Standard Book Number: 0-8225-0420-0
Library of Congress Catalog Card Number: 79-1462

2 3 4 5 6 7 8 9 10 85 84 83 82 81 80

CONTENTS

The Pacific Ocean provides a grand background for an old-car competition at Pebble Beach, California

INTRODUCTION

A rumble is heard in the distance. Out of the fog looms a Duesenberg, its polished chrome reflecting the gray morning sky. The next arrival is an elegant Rolls-Royce, still running as silently as when it was new. Here comes a pickup truck towing a trailer. On the trailer is an old Bentley racing car, as brilliantly polished as it was in its days of former glory. Soon, more and more cars arrive like ghosts out of the past.

The occasion that brings all these old cars together is an old-car competition. Already a small crowd of spectators has begun to mill around. By mid-afternoon, thousands of people will have come to share in the excitement and beauty of the event. What is so fascinating about a display of old cars that brings people together from thousands of miles around?

"They don't build 'em like they used to!" This often-heard comment is perhaps one reason why people are drawn to old cars. There are other reasons, too. Many people are attracted to the beauty of an old car gleaming with brilliant paint and brasswork. For other people, the majesty of an old car powered

7

Batteries in compartments at either end of this 1913 Broc
supplied electric current to the motor under the floor.

**The tiller in front of the driver's seat
of the Broc was for steering.**

an engine of 12 or even 16 cylinders creates
a feeling of nostalgia. Still others admire the
engineering novelties that make many of the
cars of the past well worth owning today.
Electric cars, like this 1913 Broc, for instance,
carried their owners in silence and comfort
with virtually no pollution.

Old cars show the individual handwork
that gives them a character all their own.
In modern times of mass production, when
thousands of identical cars pour off assembly
lines, it is no wonder that more and more
people dream about owning a unique car
from the past.

This 1910 Rolls-Royce was originally owned by the Prince of Wales, who later became King Edward VIII of England. He used this car to take hunting parties into the countryside.

THE DIFFERENT KINDS OF OLD CARS

In general, an old car is anything that is not a new car. But, obviously, there is a lot of difference between a 1958 Ford and a 1928 model. To distinguish among the various kinds of old cars, owners and car clubs have set up a system of classification. Cars are divided into distinct categories on the basis of their ages as well as other characteristics. There are three main types of old cars: *antique cars, classic cars,* and *special interest cars.*

ANTIQUE CARS

As their name implies, antique cars are the very oldest automobiles. The Antique Automobile Club of America had long defined antique cars as those cars built before 1930. But more recently, the club has awarded antique status to cars 25 years old or older.

The very early antique cars were experiments in self-propelled transportation. They were built by hand, one at a time. These early

This 1899 Velo was built by Karl Benz, whose company today makes the well-known Mercedes-Benz.

cars were powered by steam and electricity, and later by gasoline. Because the earliest cars were the first road vehicles that were not horse-driven, they are often called "horseless carriages."

The very first experimental automobiles did, in fact, look much like carriages. They were open-bodied vehicles, such as this 1899 German Velo. Like other early antique cars, the Velo was steered by a tiller — a rod that came up through the floor — rather than by a steering wheel. Sometime in this Velo's long life, one of its owners decided to improve the car's appearance by chrome-plating the wheel spokes and all the brass trim. The single-cylinder engine is original, however. The large copper boxes on the sides of the engine compartment are the radiators for the cooling system.

Cars continued to develop rapidly through 1929, but by 1910, they had already begun to acquire some of the characteristics of today's automobiles. Steering wheels replaced tillers, and enclosed bodies replaced the old carriage-like construction. The 1910 Rolls-Royce on page 10 shows these "modern" features.

The Velo engine

CLASSIC CARS

The cars that were built after 1925 were much closer relatives of modern cars than the ones built before. By this time, cars had acquired almost all of the features of today's automobiles, including electric starters, electric lights, and four-wheel brakes. By 1925, automotive companies had begun to use standardized parts to build their cars. As a result, most cars were no longer built one at a time by hand. Instead, they were mass produced in factories. Cars were built faster, and cheaper, than ever before.

But not all companies immediately followed the trend toward mass production. Some companies still made cars that required costly hand craftsmanship. These companies put superior engineering and beauty before price. The interiors of their special cars often had hand-built custom coach work, in which only the finest and most luxurious materials had been used. This individual attention to construction and design produced some of the highest quality cars ever built. These fine cars, built between 1925 and 1948, are called *classic cars*.

Today the Classic Car Club of America sets the exclusive standards that define a true classic car. These standards include engineering excellence, fine workmanship, elegance, and enduring design. Among those American cars currently considered classics are Auburns, Cords, Duesenbergs, Lincoln Continentals, and many Cadillacs and Packards. There are also European classics, including the Alfa Romeo, Austro Daimler, Bentley, Mercedes-Benz, and Rolls-Royce.

A sporty way to travel in 1931 was in a Cord convertible. This classic car was extremely low and sleek for its day.

This 1930 Cadillac was one of the first cars with a V-16 engine.

This 1930 Cadillac is a fine example of an American classic car whose builders spared no expense in attaining luxury and quality engineering. The car's engine, which has 16 cylinders, was the largest in its day. Cadillac owners were proud of their powerful vehicles and they kept their engines as polished as the cars' exteriors. Cadillac manufacturers

The Cadillac's engine, driver's seat, and spacious passenger compartment (with jump seat folded down)

supplied oil cans as standard equipment, so that the owners could keep their precision-made machines running like fine watches.

The interior of the 1930 Cadillac is spacious and luxurious. The car's instruments are set into a decorated stainless steel panel. Highly polished wood surrounds the windows. The car's seats are covered in fine cloth. The folding jump seats in the rear compartment can accommodate two extra people, making this a seven-passenger car. If only five people are going to ride, the jump seats can be folded down out of the way to make plenty of leg room. The back seat's center armrest can also be folded out of the way, and even the height of the rear seat cushion can be adjusted for maximum comfort.

Another American-made classic car is this 1927 Rolls-Royce. The fact that it was made in America is surprising to some people, because the Rolls-Royce typically is thought of as an English car. But some Rolls-Royces were built in Springfield, Massachusetts, from 1920 to 1931.

The trunk of this Rolls-Royce came equipped with an elegant set of silver and crystal.

Regardless of where they were made, Rolls-Royces have always stood for durability and excellent engineering. The builders of Rolls-Royces usually provided the chassis only, and the owners went to other companies for custom coachwork. The result was a quality luxury car that was lavishly decorated to the owner's taste. This 1927 model, for example, has its entire hood made of highly polished aluminum. The trunk provides a refreshment set with sterling silver and fine crystal. When this car was new, the owner would go on picnics, the trunk packed with linen tablecloths, china plates, and silver glasses.

Of all old cars, the Packard is regarded by many people as the most stately symbol of the classic era in America. For this reason, perhaps, Packards have been chosen as the

A 1927 Rolls-Royce

A 1939 Packard town car

official parade cars of many United States presidents, among them Woodrow Wilson, Warren G. Harding, Calvin Coolidge, Herbert Hoover, Franklin D. Roosevelt, and Harry Truman.

In much the same fashion, many wealthy motorists of the 1930s and 1940s were chauffeured about in elegant Packards like this 1939 Packard "town car." Town cars were direct descendants of horse-drawn coaches, in which the driver sat outside. While the town car's passengers rode in great comfort in an enclosed back compartment, the driver sat up front, exposed to the weather. For this reason, chauffeurs sometimes jokingly called the town cars "pneumonia specials." Happily for drivers, the town-car body style is no longer made.

Not satisfied with the built-in elegance of

The hood ornament of the 1939 Packard

the Packard, many owners equipped their cars with accessories to make them look even better. An example is the hand-cut crystal hood ornament on the Packard town car. It lights up when the car's headlights are turned on.

SPECIAL INTEREST CARS

Of all the cars built after 1930, only a relatively small number are considered classics. Those old cars that do not fit into the antique or classic categories are called *special interest cars*. They were the cars that most families could afford. Most old Fords, Chevrolets, and Chryslers are special interest cars.

More special interest cars survive than any other kind of old car. For this reason, special interest cars are generally less valuable than antique or classic cars. Yet special interest cars are popular collectors' items, probably because owning one is within the reach of almost any old-car enthusiast.

The value of a special interest car depends on its age and condition. Generally, the older the car, the more valuable it is. Many special interest cars are also valuable to collectors because they are no longer being made. Hudsons, Nashes, Studebakers, Kaisers, and Frazers — all these are American special interest cars that were discontinued in the 1950s and 1960s.

Each day, more fine cars are being manufactured. Like the other great cars of the past, the cars of today will become old cars with the passing of time. And some of them will survive to become the collectibles of tomorrow.

Inside an automotive showroom are several beautiful special interest cars: (from left to right) a 1954 Mercedes-Benz convertible, a 1954 Plymouth coupe with only seven miles on it, a 1952 Siata roadster, a 1955 Jaguar XK 150, and a 1931 Packard Standard Eight.

This 1929 Ford is unusual because it has right-hand drive and twin spare tires.

COLLECTING OLD CARS

For people who are really interested in old cars, few activities are more rewarding than collecting these vehicles from the past. But finding an old car may be a difficult and time-consuming process. Antique and classic cars are the most valuable to collectors, but they are also the hardest to find. Collectors often go to great expense to track them down. This 1929 Ford phaeton, for example, was found in Argentina. A phaeton is a four-door convertible with canvas side curtains instead of roll-up glass windows.

But not all collectors of old cars need a valuable antique or classic car to participate in their favorite hobby. Any old car may be a worthy subject of their time and care. Some old cars may be special because they are in nearly new condition. Others may have an unusual mechanical feature or a unique design. Some old cars warrant attention because they are rare or are no longer being manufactured. For example, convertibles are collectors' items because they are no longer being made in the United States. Even those old cars without any outstanding features may be special to some admirers. For many car fans, an old Ford, Chevrolet, or Buick can be just as much fun as a Packard, Cadillac, or Duesenberg — not only that, but it costs a lot less.

But even the least expensive old cars are getting harder and harder to find each year. Many of them were turned into scrap metal during the Second World War and the Korean War. Most of the cars that survived are already in the hands of collectors. Nevertheless, it is still possible to find an old car, even a rare one, in some abandoned garage or barn. That is the dream of every old-car collector.

Sometimes, though this very rarely happens, one may find a car, like this 1932 Austro Daimler, that has been carefully *preserved* by its owners. A preserved car is one that has stayed in its original, mint condition, often because it has not been driven much by its owners. When the Austro Daimler was purchased from its original owner in 1974, the car had been driven less than 10,000 miles in 42 years! Because they have been kept in such good condition, preserved cars are very valuable.

Most old cars are found in a state of deterioration. Years of standing idle in an unheated garage or out in the open air take their toll. An old car's engine and gears may have rusted into a solid mass. The tires may be in tatters. The body may be dented and in need of paint. In order for the owner to enjoy the car again, everything must be repaired or rebuilt. The process of fixing up a car to return it to its original condition is called *restoration*. Restoring an old car can be a long and painstaking job.

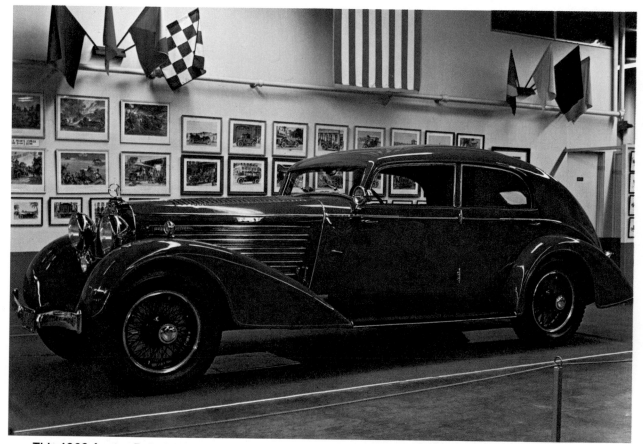

This 1932 Austro Daimler is on display at the Briggs Cunningham Automotive Museum in California.

RESTORATION

Some people restore their old cars themselves, right in their own garages or backyards. Personal restoration requires lots of time, good work space, and skilled handwork. Special shops can assist the owner with the more difficult parts of the job. There are even some shops that can do the whole restoration job from the chassis up. Most owners prefer not to leave the entire restoration job to a shop, however. They find the greatest satisfaction in being able to say, "I did it myself."

There are two kinds of restoration projects, depending on the amount of work the car needs. If the car runs reasonably well, then perhaps only "cosmetic restoration" will be needed. A car undergoing cosmetic restoration is brought up to top shape by replacing a few parts, reupholstering, and repainting, but is generally left in one piece while the work is being done on the body.

The second kind of restoration is called "complete restoration." Complete restoration is necessary if the car cannot run at all, if many of its parts are missing, or if its condition is generally a mess. In this kind of

The owner of this 1928 Lincoln limousine is installing a new set of ignition wires.

project, the car is stripped down to the bare chassis, with all of its pieces going into carefully marked containers. Then, as the car is gradually rebuilt, each piece is repaired or is replaced with an original before it is installed. In a way, complete restoration is like assembling a super-detailed, full-sized model car kit.

Most people who restore old cars, especially those who will be entering their cars in competitions, are very concerned that the changes and repairs they make on their cars are *authentic*. This means that the owners must match all of the parts on the restored car to those that would have been found on the car when it was new. Even the car's interior and accessories must be restored using the original materials. The owners cannot use modern synthetic upholstery materials, for example, no matter how much they may look like leather, because such materials may not yet have been invented when the cars were first built.

Hunting down original equipment may be frustrating for owners of very old or rare cars. Often the owners cannot find the exact item they need, so they must have a duplicate item built just for them. Here the owners must be especially careful to use exactly the same materials and design as the original manufacturer used.

Such detailed regard for authenticity means that an owner must know everything about his or her car when it was new. Luckily for the restorer, there is a lot of information available.

The mechanics in this restoration shop have removed the radiator of this 1932 Cadillac V-16 for repairs.

This 1936 Ford convertible sedan is being tuned up, and its brakes are being realigned.

This 1936 Ford Phaeton is a vintage car.

A 1934 Duesenberg with restyled fenders

Sometimes the factory that first manufactured the car can furnish technical information and exact specifications, or measurements. Another valuable reference source is a large public library that files repair and service manuals for many cars over the years. Libraries also stock back issues of car magazines, which often have drawings and photographs of cars as they looked when they were new. Sometimes an advertisement in an old magazine can answer an important question on how an item looked on the original car. Talking to owners of similar model cars is also helpful.

In the course of their research, some owners discover other kinds of restoration problems. Sometimes previous owners of a car may have altered its design or mechanical parts. To change them back to the original could be very expensive. This happened with the 1934 Duesenberg pictured here. One of its past owners thought the car looked a little old-fashioned, so he had the fenders restyled. Now the present owner is trying to decide whether he should have the car restored to its original design or keep the car in its restyled condition. It is a difficult decision.

Because restoration is such a painstaking process, it may take years before a car is completely restored. But finally the day arrives that everyone has been waiting for. Everything is done. There are no more little parts to hunt down. There is no more rust to rub out, and no more chrome to polish or replate. With a turn of the key and a press of the starter button, the engine comes to life. The proud owner can take off for a ride in a "new" old car.

An elegant lineup of classic cars at a concours. The first
three cars are a Packard, a Pierce-Arrow, and a Duesenberg.

OLD-CAR COMPETITION

All owners of old cars take great pleasure in driving their restored autos. But for some people, just driving is not enough. Many of these people join clubs where they can meet with other car fans to discuss and admire each other's cars. Some of these clubs, like the Antique Automobile Club of America and the Classic Car Club of America, host special events in which restored cars compete, and the most beautifully restored car is awarded a trophy. This special kind of old-car competition is called a *concours d'elegance*, which is a French term describing a contest or a gathering of elegance.

Since it would be unfair to put a Model A Ford up against a luxurious Rolls-Royce in a concours, the entries are divided into smaller competition classes. Cars are divided first by age into antique, classic, and special interest classes, and then by American or European manufacture. Sometimes cars are further subdivided into groups by kind or make of car, such as a Rolls-Royce or a Bentley class.

In this concours, a speedy 1931 Bentley (left) stands beside a 1928 model.

These two cars, for example, are in a separate class of Bentley racing cars. The one on the left is a 1931 model, and the one on the right was built in 1928. Both cars are painted dark green, which is Britain's official racing color. These Bentleys have other special racing features as well. The large gray object between the front wheels on the 1931 model is a supercharger. The supercharger increases the power of the car's engine. Because extra weight can slow a car down, the 1928 Bentley has a special, lightweight, leather-covered body. The car's windshield folds down for streamlining.

Even though these Bentleys were racing vehicles, they have the same fine finish as the classic Bentley passenger cars of the period. The "winged *B*" emblem, which is

The "winged B" on the radiator cap and shell marks this car as a Bentley.

Wood paneling and numerous gauges and dials make the dash of this 1928 Bentley look like the cockpit of an airplane.

a Bentley trademark, decorates their radiator shells and caps. Inside the 1928 Bentley is a handsome instrument panel that is like an airplane's. Brass dials are set into a polished wood panel.

After these Bentleys and the other cars have been parked in their competition classes, the owners and owners' friends hurry about, taking care of last-minute details before the judging starts. They check to make sure that nothing has come loose during the drive to the concours. They remove any papers that may have flown into nooks on the way. A final polishing removes every bit of dust and dirt from all parts of the car, even the engine and undercarriage. Finally the hard-working team can find no more flaws. The car is ready to be judged.

Judging is done by a team of qualified individuals who are experts in the field of automobiles. At a recent concours, for example, the judges included a man who had designed classic cars, a leading teacher of automotive styling, the owner of a car restoration shop, and the editor of an automotive magazine.

The judges score the cars on the quality of their restoration and on the elegance of their design and finish. Cleanliness, the degree of authenticity of restoration, and the general appearance of the paint, plating, trim, upholstery, and of all the working parts are checked. But appearance alone is not enough to win a concours. All mechanical parts must operate smoothly. Each car is started so that the judges can observe the working condition

This brilliantly painted car is perfectly described by the sign above it. The car is a classic Hispano-Suiza from France.

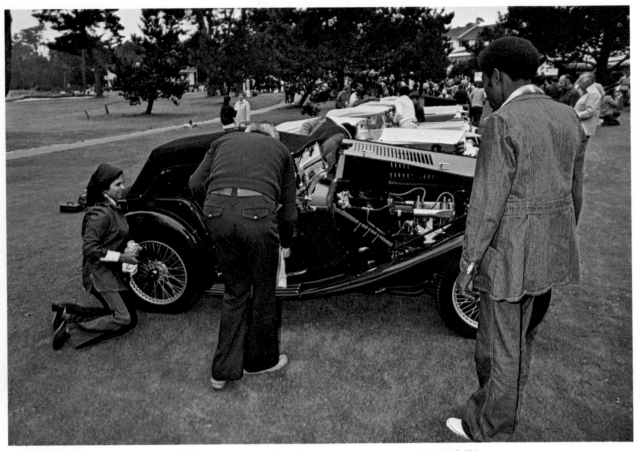

A team of judges scores an almost flawless 1937 MG TA.

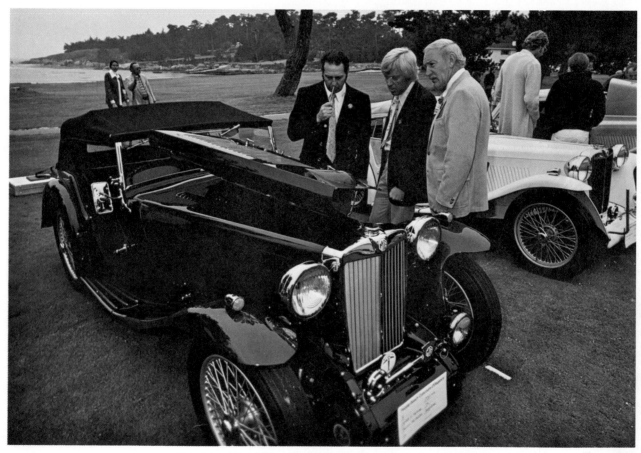

This beautiful MG will probably be awarded a trophy.

An elegant Rolls-Royce Silver Ghost rolls up onto the trophy platform at a concours.

of the engine, brakes, exhaust and cooling systems, lights, windshield wipers, and even the horn. Each item is awarded points, and the cars that have a total of 100 points after all the categories have been judged are considered perfect.

Each judge silently marks a car's point ratings on a separate score sheet. Until all of the cars have been judged, no one knows who the winners will be. Finally all of the cars are scored. The judges get together and total up the individual score sheets for each car. The three cars with the highest total point scores in each class are awarded trophies for first, second, and third place in their categories.

Then comes the hard part. The judges must pick the best car in the show from among the first-place winners in each class.

There is much comparing of notes as the judges discuss the merits of each car. Finally the judges come to a decision.

The time for awarding trophies has arrived. The crowd moves toward the presentation area. In many concourses, the winning cars drive up a platform to receive their trophies. The sparkling cars, packed with passengers sharing the excitement of the moment, make a fine sight as they slowly approach the judges' stand.

After the last car has been awarded its trophy, the owners pack up their belongings and get ready for the journey home. Some cars are loaded back onto trailers, while others are driven away. This concours is over, but there will be others. And old-car fans will have another opportunity to get together to see more fine automobiles on display.

This 1934 Packard V-12 is an early example of hardtop styling. The canvas-covered roof looks like a convertible top, but it cannot be folded down.

CONCLUSION

In this era of mass production, when car buyers are limited to the styles produced by large corporations, owning an old car has become a popular alternative. Old cars are unusual and, more important, they can be restored to reflect the owners' personal tastes. Whether an old car has the quaint look of an antique, the breath-taking beauty of a classic, or the comfortable bearing of a special interest car, it is guaranteed to draw second looks from other motorists and passersby.

But even if you cannot afford an old car of your own, you can share in the excitement of the old-car hobby. You can find old cars on display in museums or rusting away in junkyards. You can visit a concours in your area and see hundreds of old cars in their splendor and glory. You can even join a car club; it isn't necessary to own an old car to become a member of many of the major car clubs.

Discover the fun and beauty of old cars. Whether you see them in junkyards, in museums, or in parades, at a concours, or on the highway, you will be experiencing a sight that will not be quickly forgotten.

Superwheels & Thrill Sports

Airplanes
  AEROBATICS
  AIRPLANE RACING
  HOME-BUILT AIRPLANES
  YESTERDAY'S AIRPLANES

Automobiles & Auto Racing
  AMERICAN RACE CAR DRIVERS
  THE DAYTONA 500
  DRAG RACING
  ICE RACING
  THE INDIANAPOLIS 500
  INTERNATIONAL RACE CAR DRIVERS
  LAND SPEED RECORD-BREAKERS
  ROAD RACING
  TRACK RACING

  AUTO BRIGHTWORK
  CLASSIC SPORTS CARS
  DINOSAUR CARS: LATE GREAT CARS
    FROM 1945 TO 1966

KIT CARS: CARS YOU CAN BUILD
    YOURSELF
  MODEL CARS
  VANS: THE PERSONALITY VEHICLES
  YESTERDAY'S CARS

Bicycles
  BICYCLE ROAD RACING
  BICYCLE TRACK RACING
  BICYCLES ON PARADE

Motorcycles
  GRAND NATIONAL CHAMPIONSHIP RACES
  MOPEDS: THE GO-EVERYWHERE BIKES
  MOTOCROSS MOTORCYCLE RACING
  MOTORCYCLE RACING
  MOTORCYCLES ON THE MOVE
  THE WORLD'S BIGGEST MOTORCYCLE RACE:
    THE DAYTONA 200
  YESTERDAY'S MOTORCYCLES

Other Specialties
  KARTING
  SAILBOAT RACING
  SKYDIVING
  SNOWMOBILE RACING
  YESTERDAY'S FIRE ENGINES

Lerner Publications Company
241 First Avenue North, Minneapolis, Minnesota 55401